THRESHER SHARKS

The Amazing World of Sharks

BLUE SHARKS

BULL SHARKS

DEEPWATER SHARKS

FRESHWATER SHARKS

GREAT WHITE SHARKS

HAMMERHEAD SHARKS

MAKO SHARKS

RAYS

THRESHER SHARKS

TIGER SHARKS

THRESHER SHRKS

By Elizabeth Roseborough

MC MASON CREST

Mason Crest
450 Parkway Drive, Suite D
Broomall, Pennsylvania 19008
(866) MCP-BOOK (toll-free)
www.masoncrest.com

First printing
9 8 7 6 5 4 3 2 1
Printed in the USA

ISBN (hardback) 978-1-4222-4130-1
ISBN (series) 978-1-4222-4121-9
ISBN (ebook) 978-1-4222-7679-2

Library of Congress Cataloging-in-Publication Data

Names: Roseborough, Elizabeth, author.
Title: Thresher sharks / Elizabeth Roseborough.
Description: Broomall, Pennsylvania: Mason Crest, [2019] | Series: The amazing world of sharks | Includes bibliographical references.
Identifiers: LCCN 2018013893 (print) | LCCN 2018018840 (ebook) | ISBN 9781422276792 (eBook) | ISBN 9781422241301 (hardback) | ISBN 9781422241219 (series)
Subjects: LCSH: Alopiidae--Juvenile literature.
Classification: LCC QL638.95.A4 (ebook) | LCC QL638.95.A4 R67 2019 (print) | DDC 597.3--dc23
LC record available at https://lccn.loc.gov/2018013893

NATIONAL
HIGHLIGHTS

Developed and Produced by National Highlights Inc.
Editors: Keri De Deo and Mika Jin
Interior and cover design: Priceless Digital Media
Production: Michelle Luke

CONTENTS

FUN FACTS 6

CHAPTER 1 - INTRODUCING THRESHER SHARKS 9

CHAPTER 2 - THE THRESHER SHARK'S POPULATION AND HABITAT 19

CHAPTER 3 - THE THRESHER SHARK'S DIET, BEHAVIOR, AND BIOLOGY 33

CHAPTER 4 - ENCOUNTERING A THRESHER SHARK 49

SERIES GLOSSARY OF KEY TERMS 58

INDEX 60

FURTHER READING & INTERNET RESOURCES 62

AT A GLANCE 63

PHOTO CREDITS, EDUCATIONAL VIDEO LINKS, AUTHOR BIO 64

KEY ICONS TO LOOK FOR:

Words to Understand: These words with their easy-to-understand definitions will increase the reader's understanding of the text while building vocabulary skills.

Sidebars: This boxed material within the main text allows readers to build knowledge, gain insights, explore possibilities, and broaden their perspectives by weaving together additional information to provide realistic and holistic perspectives.

Educational Videos: Readers can view videos by scanning our QR codes, providing them with additional educational content to supplement the text. Examples include news coverage, moments in history, speeches, iconic sports moments, and much more!

Text-Dependent Questions: These questions send the reader back to the text for more careful attention to the evidence presented there.

Research Projects: Readers are pointed toward areas of further inquiry connected to each chapter. Suggestions are provided for projects that encourage deeper research and analysis.

Series Glossary of Key Terms: This back-of-the book glossary contains terminology used throughout this series. Words found here increase the reader's ability to read and comprehend higher-level books and articles in this field.

FUN FACTS...
GETTING TO KNOW THEM

TIGER SHARK
Named for the vertical striped markings along its body, but they fade with age.

MAKO SHARK
Known as the race car of sharks for its fast swimming speed!

BULL SHARK
Named for its stocky shape, broad, flat snout, and aggressive, unpredictable behavior!

RAYS
Rays and sharks belong to the same family. A ray is basically a flattened shark.

GREAT WHITE SHARK
With jaws this fierce, they don't call it "Great" for nothing!

BLUE SHARK
Known by their distinct blue and white coloring, their large eyes, and long snout.

HAMMERHEAD SHARK
Yes, those are eyes mounted on the side of its head, giving it 360-degree vision!

THRESHER SHARK
This clever shark uses its unique long tail fin to stun and catch prey!

WORDS TO UNDERSTAND:

bill: The long nose of a fish, such as that found on a swordfish.
breach: Often displayed during hunting, breaching is a behavior in which an aquatic animal launches its body from the water and into the air.
marine biologist: A scientist who studies the plant and animal life of the ocean.

CHAPTER 1

INTRODUCING THRESHER SHARKS

The long tail and big eyes make the thresher shark recognizable.

From its large eyes to its incredibly long, weapon-like tail, thresher sharks are some of the most recognizable predators in the ocean! When we think of sharks, we think of fierce predators with row after row of razor-sharp teeth. While the thresher shark is an amazing hunter, it's a little bit different than most other sharks, especially when it comes to how they hunt their prey. The thresher shark is special—instead of using its jaws as its primary weapon, threshers hunt with their enormous tails. With tails up to 10 ft. (3 m) long, the thresher shark has a powerful weapon directly attached to its body. Their tails, also known as their caudal fins, are usually equally as long as the rest of their bodies.

Thresher sharks use their enormous tails like whips to herd schools of fish into a small area and then stun their prey before they deliver the final blow with their jaws. Often, the whipping motion a thresher shark creates with its tail allows the shark to kill multiple fish at one time. Sometimes, the blow delivered by the tail is so powerful that it actually breaks the prey into pieces, creating less work for their small jaws. Thresher sharks do not have the impressive, large jaws that are so often seen on other sharks, but that does not stop them from being incredible hunters. Their smaller jaws require them to take multiple bites of their food. This is why it's helpful for them to kill many fish at once. After expending the energy required for the hunt, they back up and then sprint toward their dead or stunned prey to finish the job.

Thresher sharks are warm-blooded animals. This means that just like humans, they are able to control their body temperature from within, instead of relying solely on the environment around them to dictate how hot or cold they become. Thresher sharks are able to adapt to almost any environment, but they prefer and are most commonly found in tropical and temperate waters around the world. When thresher sharks are found in colder waters, it's likely because they are following a food source or looking for a mate. Male and female thresher sharks do not interact with each other except for during mating season. Threshers tend to migrate to follow warm masses of water. This migration is even more likely when they are young.

Thresher sharks use their long tails to hunt their prey.

SIDEBAR

WHERE DID THE NAME "THRESHER SHARK" COME FROM?

The thresher shark's scientific name, *Alopias vulpinus*, comes from the Greek word for fox. A few people still refer to thresher sharks as fox sharks today. Thresher sharks do not look like foxes—they got this name because even hundreds of years ago, there were many myths about their clever behaviors (such as figuring out how to free themselves from fishing lines and temporarily swallowing their babies in order to protect them from potential predators), and those who believed these myths likened these actions to those of a clever fox.

There are historical myths that thresher sharks have worked together with swordfish to kill whales, but most **marine biologists** agree that this is just a legend. The legend says that a swordfish would position itself underneath the whale with its sharp **bill** pointing upward, while the thresher shark attacked from the top, impaling the whale with the swordfish's bill. The main reason that marine biologists believe that this is unlikely is not because the thresher shark lacks the intelligence to initiate such an attack, but because both thresher sharks and swordfish lack the jaws that would be necessary to eat a whale after the kill. The current, common name of thresher shark comes from the way the shark uses its tail to hunt, whipping it around to kill prey, much like farmers use threshers to slice their crops.

The thresher shark's tail resembles a farmer's hand scythe.

Thresher sharks only mate one or two times over the course of their twenty-year lifespan, as they typically take six to eight years to reach maturity. Thresher shark babies, or pups, are typically born four at a time. The pups are not raised by their parents—they are usually on their own from the time their mother gives birth to them. It's hard to say exactly how thresher pups learn to hunt, as neither parent sticks around after birth, and they do not tend to stay with their brothers and sisters for more than a few moments.

Thresher sharks are incredibly fast swimmers, easily reaching speeds of up to 30 mph (48 kmph). They are able to achieve these speeds thanks in part to their powerful tails propelling them through the water. They are often sighted **breaching** the water while hunting, sometimes with pieces of their prey in their mouths. It's unlikely to observe this behavior near the coast, as most thresher sharks prefer to swim in the deep, open ocean.

The long tail propels thresher sharks through the water at high speeds.

While thresher sharks tend to hang out alone, they have been known to hunt in small teams of two or three. Scientists are not sure what makes some thresher sharks decide to hunt alone, while others choose to hunt in groups. Most of the time, thresher sharks only come around other sharks to mate. As apex predators, thresher sharks do not have to worry about being hunted by other animals. Some sharks travel in groups for protection from predators, but this is not necessary for the thresher shark.

Watch how the thresher shark attacks a school of sardines, stunning its prey with its powerful tail before going in for the final kill. Pay special attention to the technique the shark uses to herd the school of sardines before making a move.

SIDEBAR

ARE THRESHER SHARKS AGGRESSIVE TOWARD HUMANS?

While thresher sharks may look scary, they appear to have no interest in attacking humans! Many people who have dived with thresher sharks report that they are shy, cautious animals, who are more worried about being hurt by humans than about moving in for an attack. There has only been one documented case of a thresher shark attacking a human. The shark attacked because the human grabbed the shark's tail.

There was recently a report of a thresher shark acting aggressively toward an underwater hunter who was trying to attack the shark with a spear. It's likely that thresher sharks are willing to become aggressive when they feel threatened, but otherwise, they seem to have little desire to interact with humans. There is a widespread rumor that a thresher shark once used its tail to take the head off of a fisherman who was leaning over the edge of a boat, but no one has ever been able to prove this claim, and most marine biologists agree that it's highly unlikely that a thresher shark would do this. There have also been four reports of thresher sharks attacking fishing boats, but in each of these incidents, the people on board the boat were attempting to kill the shark. Bottom line: humans and thresher sharks have no problem peacefully coexisting as long as the shark is treated with respect.

Thresher sharks and humans can coexist.

Even though thresher sharks are not likely to be harmed by other animals, they are often harmed by humans. Thresher sharks are often hunted for their fins and their meat, and it's caused their population to decline severely. Thresher shark fins and meat are very valuable in some areas, and fishermen know that they can get a lot of money for these items. There are also companies that advertise adventure fishing—these companies attempt to lure vacationers into sport fishing for thresher sharks, as they are difficult to catch and often put up a fight. Some fishermen engage in the typically illegal practice of shark finning, in which a shark's dorsal (top) fin is removed while the shark is still alive. The finless shark is then returned to the ocean. While this sounds more humane than killing the shark, the opposite is true— sharks who have been finned either starve to death or die from their injuries.

Currently, thresher sharks are listed as vulnerable—this is the step below endangered. It's important that humans come together and protect thresher sharks, as they are an important part of keeping the ocean's ecosystem healthy.

Like other sharks, thresher shark fins are in demand as a delicacy in shark fin soup.

There is still a lot that marine biologists need to learn about thresher sharks. We currently know of three varieties of thresher sharks, but evidence suggests that there may be a fourth type. Through diving with sharks, tagging, and observing, scientists are learning more every day. Thresher sharks are particularly hard to study because they do not usually swim near the surface of the ocean unless they are hunting. There are some areas of the world that thresher sharks are known to visit regularly, particularly in the Philippines. Many scientists are working in these areas to learn as much about thresher sharks as possible. The more that scientists know about what thresher sharks need, how they behave, and what they like to eat, the easier it is to keep them safe and increase the number of threshers living in the wild.

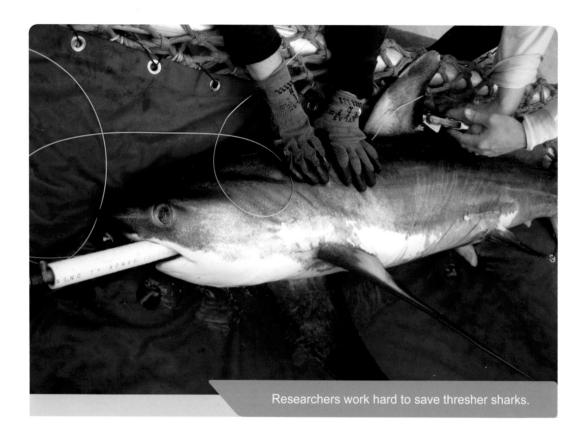

Researchers work hard to save thresher sharks.

TEXT-DEPENDENT QUESTIONS:

1. How does the thresher shark hunt?

2. Where does the name thresher shark come from?

3. How fast can thresher sharks swim?

RESEARCH PROJECT:

Research the fastest land animals and the fastest ocean animals and compare them. Which group can move faster?

WORDS TO UNDERSTAND:

bycatch: Animals such as dolphins, sharks, and porpoises that are caught accidentally in commercial fishing nets. Bycatch animals typically are either killed by fishermen or die from the injuries caused by the fishing nets.

parasite: A living thing that lives in or on another living thing, called the host. A parasite steals nutrients, calories, or both from the host's body, often causing health problems.

pelagic: Ocean animals that prefer to swim in open water, far from obstacles such as coral reefs and coastlines. Most pelagic animals swim between the surface of the ocean and 1,800 ft. (550 m) below the surface.

CHAPTER 2

THE THRESHER SHARK'S POPULATION AND HABITAT

Thresher sharks swim where they can find food.

HABITAT

Thresher sharks are found all over the world. The vast majority of the time, thresher sharks are **pelagic** animals. Pelagic animals enjoy swimming in the open ocean with the option to go deep under the surface if necessary. Unlike some pelagic animals, thresher sharks do venture near the coast at times. When thresher sharks actively pursue a school of fish, they have been known to follow the school almost anywhere.

Thresher sharks only come near the surface of the water to hunt. Most of the time, they prefer to stay in fairly deep water, typically around 1,800 ft. (550 m) deep. Found in tropical and subtropical waters, thresher sharks prefer to be warm. They will, however, venture into colder waters if food is scarce in the warmer waters they usually enjoy. The thresher shark's body allows it to adapt to colder temperatures if necessary without causing the shark to get sick or injured.

There is not a specific area in the world in which thresher sharks are most common. Threshers are happy to travel the globe, as long as they're able to stay in their desired water temperature.

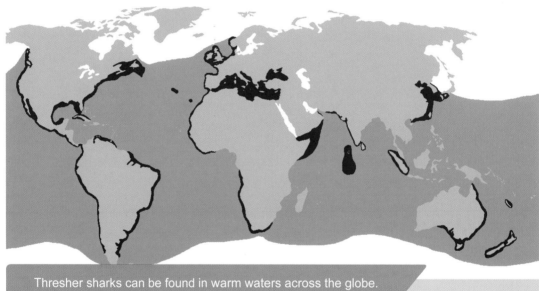
Thresher sharks can be found in warm waters across the globe.

MIGRATION

Thresher sharks migrate seasonally. In warmer months, they tend to travel north to cooler waters. When the water begins to take on the chill of autumn, thresher sharks will return to warmer waters near the equator. Thresher sharks are able to recognize when a warm area of water is traveling, and they often move with that warm body of water.

The thresher shark may very well be the strangest looking shark in the world, with a tail almost as long as its body.

Along their journeys, thresher sharks must visit cleaning stations in order to stay healthy. Cleaning stations work like car washes for sharks and other large fish. Scientists are not completely sure how thresher sharks find these cleaning stations, but it's clear that sharks know these stations are common near coastlines. While thresher sharks typically swim far from humans, they are willing to venture closer than normal when a cleaning station is nearby. From time to time, **parasites** latch onto the gills of large fish. This can become problematic as these parasites can cause infection in the gills, making breathing difficult. While sharks do not breathe in the same way that people do, it's still essential that they get enough oxygen into their blood to sustain their bodily processes. When a shark's gills become clogged with parasites, they can experience breathing difficulties that are similar to what a person with asthma experiences during an asthma attack. If these breathing issues become severe for the shark, it can lead to illness or death. In order to get rid of these parasites, sharks visit cleaning stations where small fish remove and eat parasites from their gills. The sharks seem to know that the smaller fish are helping them—they do not attack the smaller fish. They simply let them do their job of removing the parasites.

Thresher sharks rely on smaller fish to keep them free from parasites.

POPULATION

Slowly but surely, the thresher shark population is declining worldwide. There are a variety of reasons for this decline, such as sport fishing, commercial fishing, shark finning, and injuries caused by commercial fishing nets. Luckily, many people and governments are aware of this population decline and are working to make sure that thresher sharks stay around for years to come. It's important that everyone does his or her part to protect and increase the thresher shark population.

CONSERVATION STATUS

Thresher sharks are currently classified as vulnerable, which is the step before being classified as endangered. This means that over time, the global population of thresher sharks has been going down. There are a few different reasons why the population of thresher sharks has taken a nosedive, and there is a lot of work to be done to ensure that these animals do not become extinct.

Catching and tagging thresher sharks can help save them.

WHO DECIDES IF AN ANIMAL IS ENDANGERED? ARE THERE DIFFERENT LEVELS OF ANIMAL ENDANGERMENT?

The International Union for Conservation of Nature (IUCN) is an organization that works to protect plants and animals that are in danger of being eliminated from the earth. They study animals and plants with declining populations, and make recommendations on how to revitalize these populations. The IUCN has a system that determines how likely different species are to become extinct based on the trends of the species' population over recent years.

The IUCN has nine different categories of conservation status for plants and animals. The lowest two categories are not evaluated (NE) and data deficient (DD). These categories contain plants and animals that are so abundant that scientists are not currently studying their population numbers. The next category is least concern (LC). A plant or animal in this category is being watched, but is not currently at any risk of becoming extinct. The next category is near threatened (NT). Animals and plants in the NT category are likely to become extinct in the future if corrective action is not taken. Next is vulnerable (VU), and organisms in this category are close to becoming extinct, and corrective action must be taken to ensure that these populations do not disappear. The following category is endangered (EN). Animals and plants in this category are going to become extinct if current human behavior toward their species continues. Endangered animals and plants are dangerously close to disappearing from the earth. The next step is critically endangered (CR), which means that the species is incredibly close to becoming extinct in the very near future, and unless extreme corrective action is taken, disappearance is inevitable. The final two categories are extinct in the wild (EW) and extinct (EX). Species that are extinct in the wild exist in captivity, but not in the natural world. While this may seem promising, often, the animals in captivity have become used to human care and are unable to ever survive in the wild. Animals in captivity also tend to be less healthy and have shorter lifespans than animals in the wild, regardless of how scientists attempt to replicate their natural diet and habitat. Plants and animals that are extinct no longer exist.

Extinct (EX)
Extinct in the Wild (EW)
Critically Endangered (CR)
Endangered (EN)
Vulnerable (VU)
Near Threatened (NT)
Least Concern (LC)
Data Deficient (DD)
Not Evaluated (NE)

THREATS

Fishing & Shark Finning

In many areas of the world, thresher sharks are fished for sport. This means that sport fishing companies advertise deep sea shark fishing trips, and people pay the company to go out on their boat and fish for sharks. These companies make money off of killing sharks multiple times a day every day. Often, the sharks are killed as trophies, and their meat is not used. Often during sport fishing, the shark is severely injured or killed in order for the fishermen to take a photo with their catches, and then the shark's body is tossed back into the ocean. In some areas of the world, this type of fishing is illegal.

While thresher sharks are often fished for sport, they are also often fished for by people who are trying to make money off of their meat and fins. In many areas of the world, thresher shark meat is highly valued. Food supply companies know that shark fin soup is valuable, and they are willing to pay fishermen a high sum in order to obtain quality shark meat. Often, shark meat is sold on the black market—this means that the sale is not reported to the proper authorities. Companies do this so that they can earn a profit on shark meat without getting in trouble for breaking the law. When companies get caught selling meat on the black market, they are severely penalized and may lose their fishing licenses.

Shark fins and tails are often sold illegally.

Sometimes, fishermen engage in a process called finning. When a shark is finned, its top fin is removed and then sold for profit. The still-living shark is then returned to the water. While this may sound like it's more humane than killing the shark, the opposite is actually true. Without its dorsal fin, the shark is unable to swim and hunt, and will eventually either bleed to death, starve to death, or die from an infection caused by unsanitary removal of the fin. It's important to note that shark fishing companies do not engage in this practice with the idea that they are being more humane to the shark than they would be if they simply killed the shark. Fishing companies are less likely to get caught transporting individual shark fins than transporting entire bodies, and finning makes it easier for them to get the fins back to shore.

Commercial Fishing Nets

Often, thresher sharks and commercial fishing companies are hunting the same fish—specifically, tuna. When the thresher shark charges into a school of tuna, it's easy for the shark's tail to get caught in the net hanging off of the fishing boat. The thresher shark's tail is incredibly important to its well-being.

Without a tail, the thresher shark will almost certainly die, as the shark will no longer be able to hunt, and will struggle to stay afloat in the water. Sometimes, the shark can untangle itself from the net, but often, the shark ends up on board the boat, where it is killed. Thresher sharks can become aggressive if they are brought on board boats, especially if they've been injured. Once the shark is on board, fishermen often feel that they have no choice but to kill the shark, as it is seemingly impossible to get the shark back into the ocean without the fishermen sustaining injuries. Even if the shark is able to untangle itself while it's still in the water, it's often left with life threatening injuries that eventually cause the shark to die.

Unfortunately, it's hard to know exactly how many thresher sharks are victims of commercial fishing nets each year. Many commercial fisheries do not report **bycatch**, even though they are required to do so by the government. This underreporting is due to the fact that companies are often fined or penalized for bycatch.

This young thresher shark became bycatch, but fishermen released it back into the ocean.

HOW DO SCIENTISTS STUDY THRESHER SHARKS?

Scientists are just beginning to learn more about thresher sharks! The first thresher shark was tagged in 2015 off the coast of the Philippines. Thresher sharks are difficult to study because they swim in deep ocean water far from the coastline. While attaching a tag to a shark's dorsal fin causes temporary discomfort for the shark, the tag allows scientists to learn about the sharks and decide what needs to be done to keep these creatures safe. Tagging helps scientists learn about habitat, behavior, and threats, and will eventually allow them to create a conservation plan to help get thresher sharks off of the vulnerable species list.

HOW TO HELP

It can feel frustrating to read about people harming sharks, but luckily, there are many things that you can do to help shark populations grow.

Write Letters

Find out who the lawmakers are in your nearest ocean area, and write them letters explaining the importance of protecting shark populations. Tell your local lawmaker why protecting sharks is so important. Explain the importance of sharks to the ocean's ecosystem, and ask your lawmaker to create strict laws against harming sharks. You can also ask your science teacher if you can talk to your class about why sharks are important, and then have your classmates write letters as well.

Educate Others

Many people have the idea that sharks are bad, and that the fewer sharks exist, the better. This could not be further from the truth. There are many ways that you can educate others on the importance of sharks. Sharks are an important part of the ocean's ecosystem. Without sharks, other animal populations would grow out of control, eventually causing many animals to starve to death because of a lack of food. Talk to your science teacher about doing a presentation in class on why sharks matter. When you hear friends talking about being afraid of sharks, explain to them that sharks rarely attack humans, and talk to them about why sharks are important.

One way to help save sharks is to avoid restaurants that sell shark fin soup.

Make Informed Purchase Choices

There are a few ways to influence the fishing industry to better its treatment of sharks, simply by putting thought into your purchases. When you're on vacation, it's important that you do not purchase shark teeth as a souvenir. Often, these items are not authentic. If they do happen to be real, it's likely that a shark was killed or harmed in order for the seller to obtain the teeth.

When you go out to eat at a nice restaurant, look at the menu carefully. If the restaurant serves shark fin soup, it's a good idea to ask your parents if you can choose a different place to eat. When restaurants lose business, it forces them to take a close look at their menus. You can write the restaurant a letter telling them about why you disagree with serving shark fin soup. It's possible that the restaurant owners may not be aware of the environmental implications of shark fishing.

When you or your parents purchase fish to eat, it's important to check the fish company's website and make sure that they use safe fishing practices that do not result in bycatch. Check the internet resources section of this book for a website that will help you learn more about companies and their fishing practices.

You can help save sharks by not purchasing anything with shark teeth.

TEXT-DEPENDENT QUESTIONS:

1. What's one thing you can do to help keep sharks safe?

2. What is a cleaning station? Why is it important for thresher sharks to visit cleaning stations while they migrate?

3. Why are commercial fishing nets dangerous for thresher sharks?

RESEARCH PROJECT:

Many large fishing companies are changing their fishing practices to reduce bycatch. Find a fishing company that has committed to reducing bycatch and learn more about how they are making the ocean a safer place for sharks.

WORDS TO UNDERSTAND:

apex predator: An animal at the top of its habitat's food chain, meaning it has no known predators.

cavitation: A process in which a liquid is moved so quickly that boiling occurs, causing small bubbles to appear.

endotherm: Animals that are capable of controlling their own body temperature, such as humans, cats, dogs, and some sharks.

CHAPTER 3

THE THRESHER SHARK'S DIET, BEHAVIOR, AND BIOLOGY

DIET

Thresher sharks typically eat smaller pelagic fish, specifically those that swim in schools, such as bluefish, butterfish, mackerel, juvenile tuna, and cuttlefish. These bony fish make up 97 percent of a thresher shark's diet. Occasionally, thresher sharks will eat crustaceans, such as shrimp. Rarely, thresher sharks have been known to attack large seabirds, smacking them with a powerful whip of their tails before going in for the kill.

Thresher sharks typically eat smaller fish like these mackerel.

BEHAVIOR & HUNTING

Typically, thresher sharks are solitary animals. They prefer to swim alone. There have been reports of thresher sharks working in groups of two or three to hunt, but this behavior is rare. Since thresher sharks are true **apex predators**, they do not depend on other sharks for protection.

Thresher sharks are incredible hunters, and scientists are finally beginning to fully understand how they hunt. Much like a sheepdog herding a group of sheep, thresher sharks often swim in circles around the schools of fish upon

Thresher sharks use their long tails to stun their prey.

which they intend to prey, herding them into tight circles. They use their long tails to trick and confuse their prey, often disorienting many fish at one time. After their prey is confused, thresher sharks will repeatedly strike the fish with their powerful tails, stunning the prey until it is disabled and incapable of moving. The thresher shark does this by speeding up toward its prey, and then using its powerful pectoral fins to stop short. Once the shark has come to a complete stop, it lunges its head toward the ocean floor, causing its tail to whip over its head at speeds of up to 30 mph (48 kmph)!

Once the prey has been rendered immobile, thresher sharks will back up and launch themselves toward their prey with great speed, taking a bite at the end of each launch. They repeat this process until they are finished eating their prey. Since thresher sharks do not have mouths stacked with teeth like most sharks, it can take them many bites to finish eating.

Hunting in this way can be tiring for sharks—they only accurately hit their prey about a third of the time. The fact that successful strikes reward them with a large amount of food makes the energy expenditure worth it. The thresher shark's tail moves so quickly and creates so much friction with the water around it that scientists have observed small bubbles forming during the shark's strike. This process is known as **cavitation**, and it's quite rare. Cavitation happens when an object moves so quickly in the water that the water cannot keep up. This is another testament to the incredible speed and power of the thresher shark's tail.

DO OTHER ANIMALS HUNT WITH THEIR TAILS?

Attack with a tail is extremely rare in the animal world, but it isn't unheard of. Of course, some animals—such as scorpions, bees, and wasps—sting with their tails, but it's not very common for animals to use their non-stinging tails to kill their prey. Along with thresher sharks, killer whales and dolphins have been known to attack from their backsides, using their tails as a weapon.

BIOLOGY

Body

Thresher sharks have a cylindrical, torpedo-shaped body that allows them to propel themselves through the ocean at amazing speeds. Including its tail, a thresher shark can grow up 20 ft. (6 m) in length and can weigh up to 1,000 lbs. (approximately 450 kg).

The top of a thresher shark's body can range from blue to gray to black in color, depending on the species. Their sides range from silver to copper-colored, and their bellies are typically bright white. Like many sharks,

Thresher sharks have long, torpedo-like bodies.

this coloring allows the thresher shark to blend in with its surroundings. This coloring is known as countershading. When viewed from below, the thresher shark's belly allows it to blend in with the sky above, making it nearly invisible to other animals. When viewed from above, its dark coloring allows it to blend in with the ocean floor below, allowing the shark to move around undetected by animals (and humans) on the ocean's surface.

Unlike most sharks, thresher sharks are warm-blooded, or **endotherms** (just like humans). The capability to control their own body temperature gives them a great advantage when it comes to survival in the ocean, as this allows threshers to follow food into areas that are much colder than their normal habitats.

Thresher sharks have a long, red strip of muscle that runs down each side of their bodies. This muscle helps them to maintain their body heat, as it contains a network of tiny red blood vessels that lead back to the inside of the shark. This muscle also contributes to their impressive speed while hunting, and enables thresher sharks to swim for long periods of time without getting tired. Thresher sharks eat when the opportunity presents itself, so it's important that they are able to generate bursts of energy whenever a school of fish swims by—even if that happens more than once in a day.

Lateral Line

Like most fish, thresher sharks have an incredibly useful organ system known as the lateral line. The lateral line is a system of organs that sharks use to detect motion in the water, even when the motion is happening far away. This is important because it alerts sharks to potential prey around them, as they can detect movement of the prey long before it comes into the shark's line of vision. For many years, scientists thought that sharks' keen sense of smell was the most important trait in making them excellent hunters. Now, scientists are giving more of that credit to the lateral line, as it's become clear that sharks are able to learn about their prey long before they are able to see or smell it.

The lateral line stretches across the entire length of the shark's body.

Running from the top of a shark's head, around its eyes, and down to its tail, the lateral line encompasses a shark from its nose to the tip of its tail, making the shark's entire body an expert at detecting when potential prey is nearby. The lateral line is located just below the shark's skin, which allows the tiny hair-like cells in the fluid-filled line to be as close as possible to the water. These tiny cells then send messages to the shark's brain, helping it figure out where to find its next meal based on water movements. The fact that the lateral line runs the entire length of the shark's body is important. If the shark gets hurt, or a part of the line becomes damaged, it is large enough to continue working efficiently.

Many fish, including sharks, use the lateral line in conjunction with their senses of smell to figure out what is happening in the world around them. While this is helpful for detecting when prey may be nearby, it's also helpful in figuring out when a potential mating partner may be in surrounding waters.

While most sharks do have fairly good eyesight, they mainly depend on the lateral line and their senses of smell to navigate through life in the ocean.

SIDEBAR

WHAT ARE THE DIFFERENT TYPES OF THRESHER SHARKS?
Scientists know of three different types of thresher sharks: the common thresher, the pelagic thresher, and the bigeye thresher. It's likely that a fourth type of thresher shark exists! An unidentifiable shark was found off the coast of Southern California in 1995, and according to DNA analysis, the shark was a new type of thresher. Scientists have not found any more of this new type of thresher yet, but they are looking to learn more about this mysterious fourth type of shark.

Jaws

In comparison to many other species of sharks, the thresher shark's jaw is very different. Unlike their great white cousins with many rows of teeth, the thresher shark has a weak bite and its mouth only contains about eighty teeth. The teeth are small and blade-like, with smooth edges. While they are quite sharp, there simply are not enough teeth to make the shark's jaws an effective hunting tool. This is why the thresher shark must rely on its amazing strength to stun its prey with its tail before going in for the final kill.

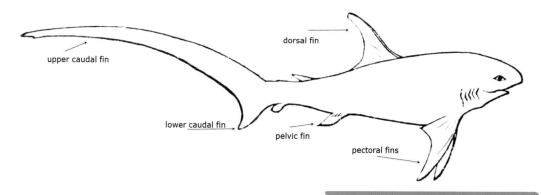

upper caudal fin

dorsal fin

lower caudal fin

pelvic fin

pectoral fins

A shark's fins keep it alive.

Fins

The thresher shark is most clearly recognized by its incredibly long upper caudal fin. The lower caudal fin is a fraction of the size of the upper lobe. Their pectoral fins (the arm-like fins on the lower front area of the shark) are small and marked with white blotches at the base. Sometimes, this white coloring extends as far as the head. The thresher's pelvic fin (located on the underside of the shark) is typically small and dark.

Tail

The thresher shark's most defining feature is its tail! Many scientists compare the thresher shark's tail to a sickle that farmers use to cut down crops. While the thresher's tail is not sharp like a sickle, it is certainly just as lethal. Scientists are only recently beginning to fully understand how the thresher shark uses its tail. It was once thought that thresher sharks simply moved their bodies from side to side to use their tails as whips, but now, scientists understand that this is far from the truth. When hunting, thresher sharks bend their entire bodies into a U shape, flipping their heads toward the ocean floor while whipping their flat, broad, pointed tails up at their prey. Like the rest of the thresher shark's body, the tail is made from cartilage, making it strong and powerful, yet flexible and light.

Watch as the thresher shark uses its incredible six-foot-long tail to devastate its prey during a hunt.

Staying Afloat

Most fish have a swim bladder—an organ filled with air that assists them in staying afloat. Sharks have no such organs, so they must rely on other methods to ensure that they do not sink. This is important for a few reasons. Sharks need to constantly be moving forward to keep water flowing over their gills, which helps them keep a flow of oxygen coming into their bodies (much like breathing keeps oxygen moving into a human's body). Without this movement, it's actually possible for sharks to drown. Although sharks and other fish do not breathe air the same way humans do, they still require oxygen in order to keep their brains, hearts, and muscles functioning normally. When a shark becomes trapped, it is likely that they will suffocate due to a lack of oxygen, since water is unable to move over their gills.

Like most sharks, the thresher shark must keep swimming to breathe.

Another reason that staying afloat is important is that as a result of changing water pressure, sharks cannot go too deep into the ocean or rise to the surface too quickly. Just like people who are scuba diving, sharks need to make these changes slowly so that their bodies are not damaged by quick pressure changes. A quick rise or fall in water pressure can cause brain damage, or even death, for a shark.

A shark's liver accounts for 25 to 30 percent of its body weight, and is a huge help in keeping the shark afloat! The liver is filled with oil that is less dense than water, allowing the shark to put in less effort to lift itself up and away from the ocean's floor. If the liver were filled with something that is denser than water, it would make it more difficult for the shark to swim.

A shark's pectoral fins (the small, arm-like fins on the underside of the shark) also help to keep the shark from sinking. Flapping these fins helps lift the shark, much like a bird's wings can lift the bird into the air. It does not take

Cartilage makes sharks flexible.

a lot of energy for a shark to move these fins, as they are usually muscular and well-developed, and they provide quite a lift toward the ocean's surface. The angle of these fins means that sharks are only able to swim in a forward motion. If they need to go backward, they either drift with the current or turn their bodies around so that they are facing the opposite direction, but they are not able to simply change the direction that they flap their fins.

Sharks do not have bones. Their skeletons are made of a tough, rubbery material called cartilage. Humans have cartilage too! You can feel it at the tip of your nose and on the outside part of your ear. Cartilage is lighter and much more flexible than bone, and makes it much easier for sharks to stay afloat than if they had a heavier skeleton.

While sharks do not have control over their oily livers or their cartilage, they are able to control their buoyancy when needed, specifically by controlling the movement of their pectoral fins. They do this when they feel threatened by another animal, or by a human. By controlling their buoyancy mechanisms, they are able to appear dead for up to fifteen minutes, causing the potential source of harm to lose interest.

Ampullae of Lorenzini

Sharks have an amazing sense that humans will never be able to experience—electroreception. The ability to sense electrical signals in the water allows sharks to locate other animals, as all animals (including humans) give off small electrical charges. This helps sharks to hunt prey even when that prey is camouflaged or hidden. This ability also is helpful in navigation, as scientists believe different parts of the earth give off different levels of electrical currents. It's believed that sharks are able to use their ability to detect these currents to create a mental map that helps them during times of migration.

Located on the underside of the thresher shark's snout, the ampullae of Lorenzini allow sharks to sense electrical fields. These are small sensory organs that are made up of a large pore filled with a gel-like substance.

Tiny sensory cells line the edge of each of the pores. These sensory cells are extremely sensitive and are able to sense even the tiniest electrical fields. The sensory cells then send messages to the shark's brain about the fields. The shark's brain can then interpret the messages and use the information to hunt or travel. This is similar to how our nerve cells work. When we touch something, our sensory cells send a message about what we're feeling to our brains, and our brains interpret that information and decide what to do with it (for example, if we're touching a hot stove, our brains send the signal to stop).

Like other sharks, thresher sharks use electroreception to help them hunt.

No matter how still or hidden a living thing may be, it cannot stop itself from emitting an electrical impulse detectable by a shark. That being said, remaining still is one of the best things that a person or animal can do to avoid a shark attack. When an animal or a human is in distress, the electrical signals emitted are erratic, and it seems that these signals attract sharks. Many marine biologists believe that this is why shark attack victims are struck repeatedly, while the shark ignores other people in the water who may be attempting to help the victim.

Sharks have also been known to bite the propellers of boats, as these emit a strong electrical signal that tells the shark that the propeller is actually alive. Many people believe that sharks attack boats because they are attempting to harm those on board, but usually, this is not the case (unless those on board are attempting to harm the shark).

It's important that sharks have a way to hunt that does not make them rely on light or smell, as often, they are hunting in the dark or in waters that have been contaminated by pollutants. Their electroreception helps them to stay safe and fed no matter what is happening in the water around them.

Lifespan

Thresher sharks take many years to mature, with females reaching maturity between eight and fourteen years of age, and males reaching maturity between seven and thirteen years of age. The many years that it takes thresher sharks to reach maturity is part of the reason behind their population decline. Over the course of their lifetimes, thresher sharks only reproduce once or twice, having two to four shark pups each time.

As is the case with many sharks, it's difficult for marine biologists to determine exactly how long thresher sharks live, as they cannot survive in captivity. Most scientists hypothesize that thresher sharks live to be approximately twenty years old, although it is possible that they live much longer.

Can you spot the thresher shark?

TEXT-DEPENDENT QUESTIONS:

1. Why are the ampullae of Lorenzini important for sharks?

2. There are three features of a shark's body that allow them to remain buoyant. What are they?

3. How is the thresher shark's jaw different from the jaws of most other sharks?

RESEARCH PROJECT:

Choose one of the physical features of the thresher shark to research. Find out if this feature is common amongst other sharks, and learn more about why the feature is so important to thresher sharks in particular.

WORDS TO UNDERSTAND:

cage diving: A way to encounter sharks in which the diver is enclosed in a steel-barred cage for the duration of the dive.

captivity: A man-made habitat, such as an aquarium or zoo. Animals are not able to leave captivity unless humans release them.

chum: Bait used by people in boats to attract sharks to nearby waters. Chum is typically a combination of fish pieces, blood, and bones, and is known for its deep red color and foul smell.

free diving: A way to encounter sharks in which the diver is not enclosed, but is instead swimming in the open ocean, often tethered to a boat.

CHAPTER 4

ENCOUNTERING A THRESHER SHARK

Now that you've learned about thresher sharks, it's only natural to want to see them up close and personal! There are a variety of ways to encounter sharks, depending on your comfort level and experience. While there are many opportunities to see other varieties of sharks, thresher sharks can be hard to find because they tend to live in deeper waters. If you're lucky enough to encounter a thresher shark during a tour or dive, be sure to take pictures—it's truly a once in a lifetime opportunity!

Thresher sharks can be hard to find because they swim mostly in the deep ocean.

OBSERVING THRESHER SHARKS

Since thresher sharks are pelagic animals that prefer deep ocean water, it can be hard to observe them from a boat. There are some areas of the world in which thresher sharks are common and can be observed by boat, but you have a much better chance of seeing thresher sharks by diving with them, as they prefer to swim many meters below the surface. If you do choose to go on a shark-watching boat trip, try not to pay attention to stories of thresher sharks attacking boats! These attacks are very rare, and are almost always caused by fishermen on the boat agitating or trying to catch the sharks. When going on a shark viewing trip, remember that no company can guarantee that you'll actually see sharks. The company can do its best to attract sharks to the boat by **chumming** the waters (local laws permitting—chumming the waters is illegal in some areas), but sharks are unpredictable wild animals and do not run on a schedule.

While thresher sharks prefer to swim in deep waters, there are many other sharks that you are more likely to see on a boat trip, such as tiger sharks. If you want to see sharks in general, it might be a good idea to set your sights on sharks that are more common near the surface of the water.

Divers will often chum the water with fish bait to attract sharks.

IS SWIMMING WITH SHARKS SAFE?

It's scary to think about swimming with sharks, but people actually do just that every day! If you decide you'd like to swim with sharks, it's important that you do not try to do this on your own. You need to be accompanied by an experienced diving team so that you can stay safe. When you're deciding on a company to use for a shark dive, be sure to research its reviews and safety record online, especially if you're diving in a foreign country. It's rare that sharks attack divers—typically, sharks know that divers bring food with them, and the sharks are much more interested in eating the bait than eating the divers! There has only been one documented case of a thresher shark attacking a human, and this happened because the human grabbed the shark's tail. As long as you keep your hands to yourself during a shark dive, it's unlikely that the shark would take any interest in bothering you. Remember, no matter how rare shark attacks are, it's important that you follow the instructions of your boat crew at all times during shark observations, dives, or both.

Cage Diving with Thresher Sharks

If you're interested in diving with sharks, but don't quite feel comfortable swimming in the open ocean, **cage diving** is a great option. When you cage dive, you'll sign up in advance and meet your boat at the dock. Once you board the boat, your captain will drive you to a location known for having an abundance of thresher sharks. While you're on your way to your cage diving location, the boat staff will give you instructions on what to expect. The staff will tell you how to keep yourself safe, and they'll remind you that you need to keep your hands and feet (including all your fingers and toes!) inside the cage at all times. They'll also get you into a wetsuit and goggles, and they will give you a breathing apparatus that you'll use to breathe during the dive. It's vital to pay close attention to the instructions and ask questions if anything is unclear. The staff will also go over what to do if you begin to feel uncomfortable and decide that you'd like to exit the water early. When you arrive at your location, the boat staff may chum the waters, if local laws permit chumming. After bait is added to the water, it's usually only a short while—ten to twenty minutes—until the sharks begin to arrive. After the sharks arrive, it's time to start cage diving! You may be permitted to dive with two to three people per cage, or cage size may require that you dive individually. You'll step off of the boat and into the cage, and you'll notice that the bars of the cage are close enough together that a shark would not be able to enter the cage.

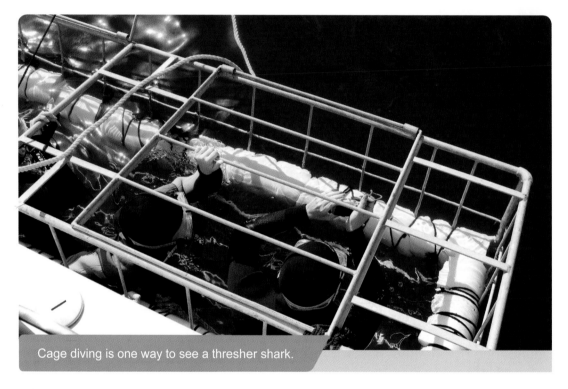
Cage diving is one way to see a thresher shark.

After you step into the cage, the boat staff will close the top and secure the latch so that it is unable to come loose. While this may make you feel claustrophobic, it's important that you're secure in the cage so that a shark cannot hurt you. Slowly, the boat staff will lower the cage into the ocean using a steel chain. You'll be lowered to a safe level where you are most likely to encounter sharks. While underwater, you can take pictures if you have an underwater camera. It's likely that the sharks you see will be curious about you and swim near your cage to get a better look!

Cage diving hasn't been around for a very long time—the method first came into practice in 1963. A shark attack survivor, Rodney Fox, came up with the idea. He wanted a way for people to experience sharks without putting themselves in harm's way. Watch this video as Rodney Fox describes his experience.

Free Diving with Sharks

If you're feeling extra brave, you may want to explore the option of **free diving** with sharks! In most cases, it takes scuba training and certification in order to become qualified to do this type of dive. You do not need to live near the ocean in order to become scuba certified—many YMCAs actually run scuba certification classes in their pools!

Once properly certified, you'll be able to dive with sharks! Shark dives are labeled as beginner, intermediate, or advanced—make sure you pick a level that you feel comfortable with. If you're unsure of whether or not you're ready to complete a dive, it's a good idea to give the diving company a call and ask a professional for his or her opinion.

Even after you're certified to dive, it's important to never dive alone. When diving in an attempt to encounter sharks, you absolutely must dive with a certified company. Sharks are unpredictable and you need to be with an expert who knows what to expect. When you board the boat, your boat captain will take you out to an area known for sharks. Just like with cage dives, if it's permitted, it's likely that the crew will chum the waters to attract sharks. Once the sharks show up, it's time to dive! Sharks may be curious about you, but it's likely they'll be more interested in looking for bait. It's important that you pay attention to your guides, as they are trained and experienced in recognizing signs of aggression and will be able to let you know immediately if the dive is becoming unsafe and you need to exit the water.

To free dive with sharks, you may need to get scuba certified.

MALAPASCUA ISLAND, PHILIPPINES

It's not always easy to find thresher sharks in the wild, as they prefer to live in the deep, open ocean. The area off the coast of Malapascua Island in the Philippines is an exception to that rule. Residents and visitors can catch glimpses of thresher sharks near the shore almost daily because of the existence of a cleaning station! Small fish hang out here to pick parasites off of the skin of thresher sharks. It's important that thresher sharks have parasites removed from their skin regularly in order to stay healthy and free from disease.

Many thresher sharks like to hang out at Malapascua Island in the Philippines.

Fishing Trips

While it can be tempting to go on a shark fishing trip, it's important to remember that these animals are a valuable part of the ocean's ecosystem. Sharks are in the ocean to help keep the environment healthy, not for human entertainment. Often, shark fishing trips encourage people to catch and kill sharks for no reason other than their own amusement. This results in the fishing company making a lot of money, the ocean being harmed, and people failing to understand how important sharks are to the ecosystem. You can take a stand for sharks and other ocean creatures by refusing to participate in shark fishing trips.

Sharks in Captivity

Like most pelagic ocean animals, thresher sharks are unable to survive in **captivity**. Pelagic animals are not used to barriers in their swimming area, and it's quite difficult for them to navigate obstacles such as walls, floors, and other animals. When confined to an aquarium, pelagic animals often injure themselves by running into barriers. It's typical for pelagic animals to become disengaged and refuse to eat, eventually starving to death, when they are confined to an aquarium tank. Hunting is a large part of a shark's life, and when they do not get to hunt as they would in the wild, it seems that food loses its appeal. While it can feel disappointing to be unable to see most sharks at aquariums, it's important to understand that existing in an aquarium setting is a death sentence for most sharks. Remember, even if you are not able to participate in seeing sharks up close, there are plenty of videos to watch that will help you study shark behavior. You can also contact your local university and ask if you would be able to sit in on a college oceanography class to learn even more about sharks

Some fishermen enjoy catching thresher sharks, but this is why thresher sharks are in danger.

It's best to see a shark in its own environment because most sharks do not survive in captivity.

TEXT-DEPENDENT QUESTIONS:

1. What does it mean to chum the waters?

2. Why do pelagic animals struggle to survive in captivity?

3. What causes sharks to attack boats?

RESEARCH PROJECT:

Thresher sharks visit cleaning stations (such as the one in Malapascua, Philippines) to stay healthy and disease free. This is called a mutualistic relationship, because both animals are getting a benefit. The thresher sharks are staying healthy, and the cleaning fish are getting something to eat. Research other animals that pair up and have a similar relationship in which both species benefit.

Apparatus: A device or a collection of tools that are used for a specific purpose. A diving apparatus helps you breathe under water.

Barbaric: Something that is considered unrefined or uncivilized. The idea of killing sharks just for their fins can be seen as barbaric.

Buoyant: Having the ability to float. Not all sharks are buoyant. They need to swim to stay afloat.

Camouflage: To conceal or hide something. Sharks' coloring often helps camouflage them from their prey.

Chum: A collection of fish guts and fish remains thrown into the ocean to attract sharks. Divers will often use chum to help attract sharks.

Conservation: The act of preserving or keeping things safe. Conservation is important in keeping sharks and oceans safe from humans.

Decline: To slope down or to decrease in number. Shark populations are on the decline due to human activity.

Delicacy: Something, particularly something to eat, that is very special and rare. Shark fin soup is seen as a delicacy in some Asian countries, but it causes a decline in shark populations.

Expedition: A type of adventure that involves travel for a specific purpose. Traveling to a location specifically to see sharks would be considered an expedition.

Ferocious: Describes something that is mean, fierce, or extreme. Sharks often look ferocious because of their teeth and the way they attack their prey.

Finning: The act of cutting off the top (dorsal) fin of a shark specifically to sell for meat. Sharks cannot swim without all of their fins, so finning leads to a shark's death.

Frequent: To go somewhere often. Sharks tend to frequent places where there are lots of fish.

Ft.: An abbreviation for feet or foot, which is a unit of measurement. It is equal to 12 inches or about .3 meters.

Indigenous: Native to a place or region.

Intimidate: To scare or cause fear. Sharks can intimidate other fish and humans because of their fierce teeth.

Invincible: Unable to be beaten or killed. Sharks seem to be invincible, but some species are endangered.

KPH: An abbreviation for kilometers per hour, which is a metric unit of measurement for speed. One kilometer is equal to approximately .62 miles.

M: An abbreviation for meters, which is a metric unit of measurement for distance. One meter is equal to approximately 3.28 feet.

Mi.: An abbreviation for miles, which is a unit of measurement for distance. One mile is equal to approximately 1.61 kilometers.

Migrate: To move from one place to another. Sharks often migrate from cool to warm water for several different reasons.

MPH: An abbreviation for miles per hour, which is a unit of measurement for speed. One mile is equal to approximately 1.61 kilometers.

Phenomenon: Something that is unusual or amazing. Seeing sharks in the wild can be quite a phenomenon.

Prey: Animals that are hunted for food—either by humans or other animals. It can also mean the act of hunting.

Reputable: Something that is considered to be good or to have a good reputation. When diving with sharks, it is important to find a reputable company that has been in business for a long time.

Staple: Something that is important in a diet. Vegetables are staples in our diet, and fish is a staple in sharks' diets.

Strategy: A plan or method for achieving a goal. Different shark species have different hunting strategies.

Temperate: Something that is not too extreme such as water temperature. Temperate waters are not too cold or too hot.

Tentacles: Long arms on an animal that are used to move or sense objects. Octopi have tentacles that help them catch food.

Vulnerable: Something that is easily attacked. We don't think of sharks as being vulnerable, but they are when they're being hunted by humans.

INDEX

A
Ampullae of Lorenzini, 43–45
apex predator, 13, 32, 34
attacks on humans, 14, 45, 50

B
behaviors, 34, 56
bigeye thresher, 39
biology, 9–10, 16, 36–45, 46*fig*, 56
    See also specific characteristics
black market, 25
body, 36–37
breaching, 8, 12
bycatch, 18, 26–27

C
cage diving, 48, 51–52, 52*fig*
captivity, 48, 56–57
cartilage, 40, 43
categories of endangerment, 24
caudal fin. *See* tail
cavitation, 32, 35
chumming, 48, 50–52
cleaning stations, 21, 54
coloration, 36–37
common thresher, 39
conservation, 22–24, 28, 55
    conservation, 16
countershading, 36–37
critically endangered animals, 24–25

D
declining numbers, 22
diet, 10, 33

E
education, 28, 56
electrical signals, 45
electroreception, 43–45
endotherm, 10, 32, 37
eyes, 9, 39

F
finning, 15–16, 22, 25–26
fins, 39, 39*fig*, 40, 42–43
fishing nets, 22, 26–27
fishing trips, 55, 56*fig*
    See also conservation; how to help;
    ocean ecosystem
Fox, Rodney, 53
free diving, 48, 53–54

H
how to help, 28–30, 55
    See also conservation
hunted by humans, 15
hunting methods, 10, 13, 19, 34–35, 43–45

I
illegal fishing, 25
International Union for Conservation of Nature
(IUCN), 24
IUCN. *See* International Union for Conservation of Nature

J
jaws, 10–11, 39

L
lateral line, 37–39
length, 36
letter-writing, 28, 30
lifespan, 45
liver, 42

M
Malapascua Island (Philippines), 54, 55*fig*
marine biologists, 8, 11, 14, 16, 28, 45
migration, 11, 20, 43–44
myths, 10

N
new type of thresher, 39

O

observing, 49–54
ocean ecosystem, 28, 55
   essential to, 16
origin of name, 11

P

parasites, 18, 21, 54
pelagic animals, 18–19, 49–50, 56
pelagic thresher, 39
Philippines, 16, 54, 55*fig*
physical description, 9–10
population, 15, 22
preferred waters, 10, 12, 18–19, 20*fig*, 49–50
pups, 12

Q

QR Video
   Appearance, 21
   Cage Diving, 53
   Hunting Sardines, 14
   Hunting with Tail, 40

R

reproduction, 12, 38, 45

S

safety, 53–54
scuba training, 53
scythe, 12*fig*
sense of motion. *See* lateral line

sense of smell, 37–38
shark fin soup, 25, 30
sidebar
   animal endangerment, 24
   hunting with tails, 35
   Malapascua Island (Philippines), 54
   swimming with sharks, 51
   tagging thresher sharks, 28
   thresher shark diet, 10
   thresher shark name, 11
   thresher shark types, 39
   thresher sharks and humans, 14
souvenirs, 29–30
speed, 12–13, 35
sport fishing, 15, 22, 25
staying afloat, 41–43

T

tagging, 28
tail, 9–10, 27, 35, 40
tiger sharks, 50
tuna, 26

U

underwater camera, 49, 52

W

weight, 36

Y

YMCA, 53

FURTHER READING:

Brusha, Joe. *Top Ten Deadliest Sharks.* Horsham: Zenescope Entertainment. 2010.

Capuzzo, Michael. *Close to Shore: The Terrifying Shark Attacks of 1916.* Portland: Broadway Books. 2002.

Eilperin, Juliet. *Demon Fish: Travels Through the Hidden World of Sharks.* New York City: Pantheon. 2011.

Lang, Heather. *Swimming with Sharks: The Daring Discoveries of Eugenie Clark.* Park Ridge: Albert Whitman Company. 2016.

Northrop, Michael. *Surrounded By Sharks.* New York City: Scholastic Press. 2014.

INTERNET RESOURCES:

http://cnso.nova.edu
The Halmos College of Natural Sciences and Oceanography provides shark videos and shark activity maps.

http://cnso.nova.edu/sharktracking
The Guy Harvey Research Institute (GHRI) Shark Tracking partners with the Halmos College of Natural Sciences and Oceanography in tracking and recording shark activity. The GHRI dedicates its resources to the preservation of marine life, including sharks.

http://www.defenders.org/sharks/basic-facts
The Defenders of Wildlife site explains how we can all do our part to increase shark populations across the globe.

https://www.discovery.com/tv-shows/shark-week/
Check out the Shark Week site from The Discovery Channel for information on all types of sharks, as well as tons of videos showing up-close shark encounters.

https://www.floridamuseum.ufl.edu/fish/discover/species-profiles
The University of Florida's Florida Museum Website provides full profiles on fish and sharks. Use this site to learn more about sharks, their behavior, and their populations.

https://www.msc.org/where-to-buy/product-finder/product_search?country=US
The Marine Stewardship Council provides up-to-date information detailing the sustainable (or not-so-sustainable) fishing practices of common seafood companies.

http://saveourseas.com
The Save Our Seas Foundation focuses their efforts specifically on saving sharks and rays. Their website includes shark facts, a newsletter, and details about how to help save sharks and rays.

AT A GLANCE

Source: www.iucnredlist.org

SWIM DEPTH

- 200 ft.
- 400 ft.
- 600 ft.
- 800 ft.
- 1,000 ft.
- 1,200 ft.
- 1,400 ft.
- 1,600 ft.
- 1,800 ft.

Hammerhead Sharks
Length: 20 ft. (6.1 m)
Swim Depth: 262 ft. (80 m)
Lifespan: 20+ years

Bull Sharks
Length: 11.1 ft. (3.4 m)
Swim Depth: 492 ft. (150 m)
Lifespan: 18+ years

Rays
Length: 8.2 ft. (2.5 m)
Swim Depth: 656 ft. (200 m)
Lifespan: 30 years

Great White Sharks
Length: 19.6 ft. (6 m)
Swim Depth: 820 ft. (250 m)
Lifespan: 30 years

Blue Sharks
Length: 12.5 ft. (3.8 m)
Swim Depth: 1,148 ft. (350 m)
Lifespan: 20 years

Tiger Sharks
Length: 11.5 ft. (3.5 m)
Swim Depth: 1148 ft. (350 m)
Lifespan: 50 years

Thresher Sharks
Length: 18.7 ft. (5.7 m)
Swim Depth: 1200 ft. (366 m)
Lifespan: 50 years

Mako Sharks
Length: 13.1 ft. (4 m)
Swim Depth: 1,640 ft. (500 m)
Lifespan: 32 years

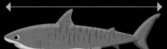

PHOTO CREDITS

EDUCATIONAL VIDEO LINKS

Chapter 1
Watch how the thresher shark attacks a school of sardines:
http://x-qr.net/1Eoi

Chapter 2
The thresher shark may very well be the strangest looking shark in the world, with a tail almost as long as its body: http://x-qr.net/1Ezw

Chapter 3
Watch as the thresher shark uses its incredible six-foot-long tail to devastate its prey during a hunt: http://x-qr.net/1FoY

Chapter 4
Watch this video as Rodney Fox describes his experience of a shark attack:
http://x-qr.net/1HSZ

AUTHOR'S BIOGRAPHY

Elizabeth Roseborough is a former college, high school, and middle school biology instructor. When not visiting her favorite Caribbean islands, Elizabeth spends her time with her husband, son, and their fur babies, Titan and Stella, at their home in Dayton, Ohio.